# THE WORLD OF DINOSAURS

# OVIRAPTOR

BY REBECCA SABELKO

EPIC

BELLWETHER MEDIA · MINNEAPOLIS, MN

T0004989

# EPIC

**EPIC BOOKS** are no ordinary books. They burst with intense action, high-speed heroics, and shadows of the unknown. Are you ready for an Epic adventure?

This edition first published in 2021 by Bellwether Media, Inc.

No part of this publication may be reproduced in whole or in part without written permission of the publisher. For information regarding permission, write to Bellwether Media, Inc., Attention: Permissions Department, 6012 Blue Circle Drive, Minnetonka, MN 55343.

Library of Congress Cataloging-in-Publication Data

Names: Sabelko, Rebecca, author.
Title: Oviraptor / Rebecca Sabelko.
Description: Minneapolis, MN : Bellwether Media, 2021. | Series: Epic : The world of dinosaurs |
Includes bibliographical references and index. | Audience: Ages 7-12 | Audience: Grades 4-6 |
Summary: "Engaging images accompany information about the oviraptor. The combination of high-interest subject matter and light text is intended for students in grades 2 through 7"-- Provided by publisher.
Identifiers: LCCN 2020014875 (print) | LCCN 2020014876 (ebook) |
   ISBN 9781644872925 (library binding) | ISBN 9781681038377 (paperback) |
   ISBN 9781681037554 (ebook)
Subjects: LCSH: Oviraptor--Juvenile literature.
Classification: LCC QE862.S3 S23245 2021  (print) | LCC QE862.S3  (ebook) | DDC 567.912--dc23
LC record available at https://lccn.loc.gov/2020014875
LC ebook record available at https://lccn.loc.gov/2020014876

Editor: Betsy Rathburn      Designer: Jeffrey Kollock

Printed in the United States of America, North Mankato, MN

# TABLE OF CONTENTS

# THE WORLD OF THE OVIRAPTOR

beak

⚠️ PRONUNCIATION

oh-vih-RAP-tor

The oviraptor was a dinosaur with feathers. It also had a toothless beak. It looked like a parrot's beak!

## MAP OF THE WORLD

**Late Cretaceous period**

### DINO NEST!

Scientists discovered the fossils of an oviraptor sitting on a nest of eggs!

The dinosaur lived during the Late **Cretaceous period**. This was part of the **Mesozoic era**.

# WHAT WAS THE OVIRAPTOR?

crest

The oviraptor had a tall **crest** on top of its head.

Some people believe the crest was used to make sounds. Others think it kept the dinosaur cool.

## SIZE CHART

15 feet (4.6 meters)

10 feet (3 meters)

5 feet (1.5 meters)

The oviraptor had a **flexible** tail. It bent and waved easily. It was covered in feathers.

Scientists think this helped the dinosaur get the attention of other oviraptors!

# DIET AND DEFENSES

⚠️ **A LIZARD MEAL**

The bones of a small lizard were found with the fossils of an oviraptor. The bones told scientists what the oviraptor ate!

The oviraptor was an **omnivore**. It used its strong beak as a tool. It could crack open hard fruits and **shellfish**. Clawed fingers helped the oviraptor catch meals. They snacked on small **mammals** and lizards.

## OVIRAPTOR DIET

shellfish

small mammals

lizards

This dinosaur did not have teeth to chew its meals. But it had spikes on the roof of its mouth. These helped the oviraptor eat.

It swallowed rocks to help grind meals in its stomach.

Large eyes helped the oviraptor
spot enemies coming near.

The dinosaur sometimes ran from **predators**. But it also attacked enemies with its beak. It slashed with its sharp claws!

# FOSSILS AND EXTINCTION

## ⚠ MISSING BONES

A full oviraptor skeleton has never been found.

A mass **extinction** began around 66 million years ago. Dinosaur bones were buried for thousands of years. They became **fossils**!

Scientists found the first oviraptor fossils in Asia in 1923. They were found in a nest. Scientists thought the dinosaur stole eggs. But they later learned the dinosaur was sitting in its own nest!

oviraptor fossil

## ⚠ EGG NAME

The word *oviraptor* means "egg thief."

# OVIRAPTOR FOSSIL MAP

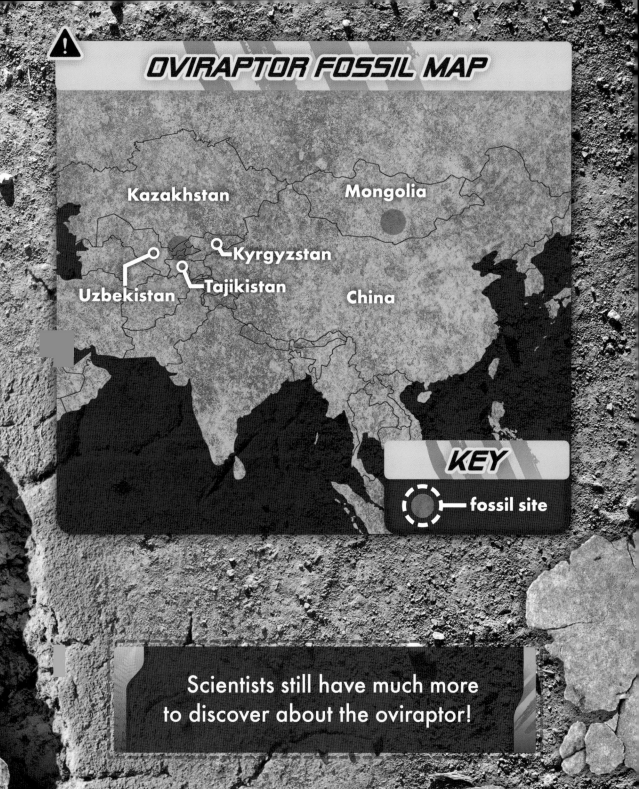

Kazakhstan

Mongolia

Kyrgyzstan

Uzbekistan

Tajikistan

China

**KEY**

fossil site

Scientists still have much more
to discover about the oviraptor!

# GET TO KNOW THE OVIRAPTOR

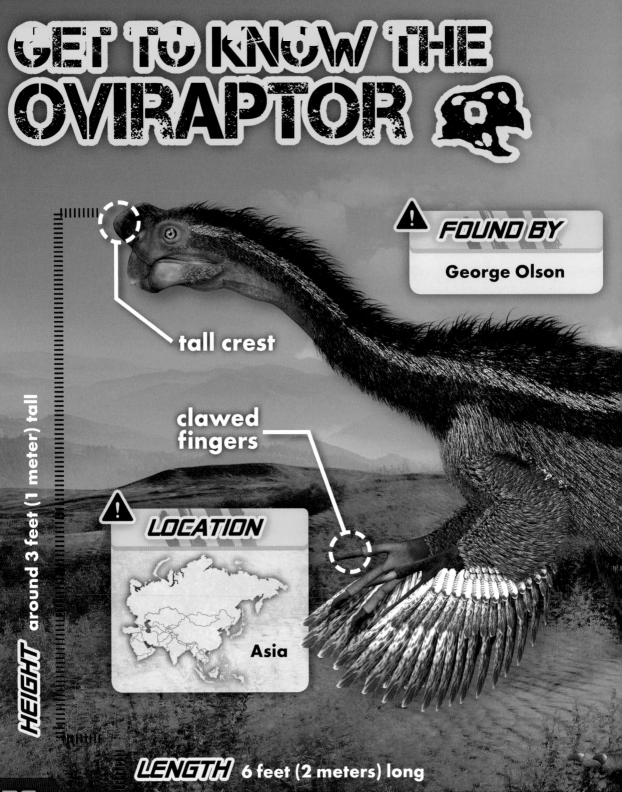

tall crest

clawed fingers

**FOUND BY**

George Olson

**LOCATION**

Asia

**HEIGHT** around 3 feet (1 meter) tall

**LENGTH** 6 feet (2 meters) long

**long tail**

⚠ **FIRST FOSSILS FOUND**

Gobi Desert in 1923

⚠ **FOOD**

lizards

small mammals

⚠ **WEIGHT**

44 pounds
(20 kilograms)

🦖 = 🦃🦃🦃

# GLOSSARY

**crest**—a showy growth on the head of an animal

**Cretaceous period**—the last period of the Mesozoic era that happened between 145 million and 66 million years ago; the Late Cretaceous period began around 100 million years ago.

**extinction**—a state of no longer living

**flexible**—able to bend easily

**fossils**—the remains of living things that lived long ago

**mammals**—warm-blooded animals that have backbones and feed their young milk

**Mesozoic era**—a time in history in which dinosaurs lived on Earth; the first birds, mammals, and flowering plants appeared on Earth during the Mesozoic era.

**omnivore**—an animal that eats both plants and animals

**predators**—animals that hunt other animals for food

**shellfish**—animals that have hard outer shells and that live in water

## AT THE LIBRARY

Braun, Eric. *Could You Survive the Cretaceous Period?: An Interactive Prehistoric Adventure.* North Mankato, Minn.: Capstone Press, 2020.

Murray, Julie. *Oviraptor.* Minneapolis, Minn.: Abdo Zoom, 2020.

Sabelko, Rebecca. *Velociraptor.* Minneapolis, Minn.: Bellwether Media, 2020.

## ON THE WEB

## FACTSURFER

Factsurfer.com gives you a safe, fun way to find more information.

1. Go to www.factsurfer.com.

2. Enter "oviraptor" into the search box and click 🔍.

3. Select your book cover to see a list of related content.

# INDEX